FAIRIES

PLAIN & SIMPLE

D1240619

FAIRIES

PLAIN & SIMPLE

An Introduction to the History and Mystery
of Their Magical Realm

RALPH HARVEY

THE ONLY BOOK YOU'LL EVER NEED

HAMPTON ROADS

Cover design by Jim Warner
Cover art: Richard Doyle, illustration from *In Fairyland*, 1870
Interior design by Kathryn Sky-Peck

Hampton Roads Publishing Company, Inc.
Charlottesville, VA 22906
Distributed by Red Wheel/Weiser, LLC
www.redwheelweiser.com
Sign up for our newsletter and special offers by going to
www.redwheelweiser.com/newsletter

ISBN: 978-1-57174-782-2
Library of Congress Cataloging-in-Publication Data available upon request

Printed in Canada
MAR
10 9 8 7 6 5 4 3 2 1

Dedication

To my loving wife, Audrey, who read and edited each page and gave much helpful advice—not to mention traversing rough and rocky countryside to explore old deserted fairy sites and investigating those wild areas where they still existed. Like myself, she was profoundly affected by the ethereal experience in that Irish valley.

To the Honorable Olivia Robertson, Grainne, Petra Ginman, Georgina Angele, Lady Levanah, and Shell Bdolack.

To the late Stewart Farrar and Lord and Lady Strathloch.

To the Pook covens, who faithfully kept the old ways and still followed the fairy path.

To the Irish Druids, who attended Audrey's initiation into the Fellowship of Isis.

I heard along the early hills,

Ere yet the lark was risen up,

Ere yet the dawn with firelight fills

The night—dew of the bramble-cup,—

I heard the fairies in a ring

Sing as they tripped a lilting sound

Soft as the moon on wavering wing.

The starlight shook as if with sound,

As if with echoing, and the stars

Franked their bright eyes with trembling gleams;

While red with war the gusty Mars

Rained upon earth his ruddy beams.

He shone alone, low down the West,

While I, behind a hawthorn-bush,

Watched on the fairies flaxen-tressed

The fires of the morning flush.

Till, as a mist, their beauty died,

Their singing shrill and fainter grew;

And daylight tremulous and wide

Flooded the moorland through and through;

Till Urdon's copper weathercock

Was reared in golden flame afar,

And dim from moonlight dreams awoke

The towers and groves of Arroar.

—Walter de la Mare, "The Fairies Dancing"

Contents

Part One

THE MAGICAL REALM OF FAIRIES

An Introduction to Fairies

At a time that is not a time,
In a place that is not a place,
And on a day that is not a day.
—OLD WICCAN ADAGE

Fashions come and go and so does belief in the things that people can and cannot see. Perfectly ordinary people experience strange things, and these events either become part of local folklore or are laughed away. What seems clear is that fairies, along with a host of other supernatural creatures, certainly do exist and that many millions of perfectly sane people hear them and sometimes see them. Stories about such creatures are common among those who live in rural areas and those whose countries are less developed. Thus, legends have been handed down in such varied places as Scandinavia, Europe, Ireland, Africa, Native American reservations, Eastern Europe, Russia, and just about everywhere else on the face of the earth. Fairies and other supernatural beings are part of the fabric of every undeveloped area on earth—and a few developed ones as well.

Research makes it clear that British, Irish, and European fairies prefer to live in woodlands, near water, and particularly near willow trees, while other countries have their own legends. After all, there are no willow trees in the African bush and precious little water, yet supernatural beings definitely live there. There may be people reading this book who live in the deserts of Australia or the United States, and if so, you may fear that there are no fairies in your area. Not a bit of it. If your area is only lightly populated, there will definitely be small supernatural beings where you live. They may be a bit dustier than their woodland counterparts, and they probably prefer to wear sandy colors rather than woodland green as a natural camouflage, but they are definitely there!

It seems that supernatural beings have certain things in common. They don't like to be disturbed by humans, although they

An artist's rendition of how we typically imagine fairies to look

tolerate children, which is why children see such phenomena far more frequently than adults do. Many supernatural creatures are mischievous, and some are downright nasty, but some like to help mankind and are said to teach certain people how to use herbs for medicine and how to use magic.

Supernatural beings are often drawn to children. (Illustration for Charles Kingsley's *The Water Babies*, by Jessie Willcox Smith, circa 1916; source Library of Congress).

Accidents will happen, and in every community children are either born with defects or don't develop properly. Many cultures believe that supernatural beings have interfered with these children in some way or even taken them away and put something strange in their place. You can imagine what happens to such children in these cultures! We know perfectly well that malevolent gnomes or hobgoblins aren't responsible for making children sick or disabled, because we understand the mechanics of these things. However, we also know what it's like to put something down somewhere only to find that it has vanished. Sometimes the "lost" article turns up again somewhere else. Legend has it that fairies take the item, play with it for a while, and then (if they are in a good mood) put it back again. This is especially the case with bright objects such as keys and jewels.

It is also perfectly possible for you to access fairies yourself and to call upon the help of a good-natured fairy or two to help you when you most need it. You will discover how to do this later in this book.

Incidentally, I have chosen to spell the word "fairy" in the most familiar way, but here are some other spellings:

Faerie

Fata (from the Latin for "fate")

Fay

Fey

Fae

"Fairy" is probably the most commonly used term for this type of supernatural being, but regional variations abound:

Region	Names for Supernatural Beings
Latin	Fata ("fata" means "the goddess of fate" and is the origin of the word "fairy")
England	Fairy • Faerie • Good folk • Elf and elves • Enchanters
London	Little people
Cornwall	Small people • Piskies
Devon	Piskies
Isle of Man	Little people • Little fellows • Children of pride
Scotland	*Sidhe* • Good neighbors • Women of peace • Still folk (as in "keeping still")
Wales	Mother's blessing • Fair family of the wood
Ireland	The gentry • *Sidhe* • *Sidthe* • Wee folk • Little red men • Good people • Honest folk • People of peace • Fair folk • Blessed folk • Hill folk
France	Godmothers • Our good mothers • Good ladies • Good neighbors
Brittany in France	*Bugul noz* (a kindly goblin)
North Germany	*Kleine Volk*
Scandinavia	*Tylwyth teg* • *Alfar*

Many Kinds of Beings

Supernatural beings can be anything from giants to trolls, dwarves, gnomes, hobgoblins, leprechauns, African tokoloshes, elves, and fairies. Judging by historical records, there are far more references to elves than to fairies. Indeed, any name that has the letters *alf*, *alv*, *elf*, or *elv* in it refers to elves. A friend of ours is called Elizabeth—her name clearly harks back to a time when elves were a common sight!

Not all these creatures are benign, and some, like the African entities, are terrifying. Even fairies can be mischievous, so if you set out to see them, you will be taking some kind of risk, although European lore suggests that they cannot do real harm to humankind.

Some magical creatures can look terrifying.

An angel—or a fairy?—carries off a baby. *Night With Her Train Of Stars*, by Edward Robert Hughes, 1912 (Birmingham Museum and Art Gallery, Birmingham, England)

Modern reports suggest that fairies and angels can be somewhat interchangeable, but others say that it is impossible to confuse the two. Those who have seen these visions say an outline of a creature may be anything from a few inches tall to ten feet high. Most reports state that the entity glows with bright light, and because it is translucent, the entity is hard to see clearly. One thing that comes through plainly from every report is the impression or feeling of a presence, and—when the being is a kindly one—a sensation of love, kindness, and warmth.

The Mystery Begins

1

*Clonegal, Enniscorthy,
County Wexford, August 1981*

As dawn broke on that momentous day in 1981, I stood on the parapet of Huntington Castle in Clonegal at Enniscorthy in Ireland and watched the gentle mist roll away over the hills, lifting as it went. Above, a strong sun blazed through, heralding a fine day.

I went down the winding dark staircase to an early breakfast and to plan the day's itinerary. Little did I realize that the events of that day in August would forever be etched in my memory and that twenty-five years later they would lead me to write this book. Despite nagging doubts in my own beliefs on the subject of fairies, and memories of my own strange experience that day in Clonegal, I hesitated about writing any more on the subject of fairies. Then I became aware of an ancient law—one that still had not been repealed—making it a capital offense to kill a fairy! The law, which Henry III had passed in 1153, stated that even the wounding or maiming of a fairy could bring about the death penalty, such was the reverence in which these creatures were held!

My wife and I spent five weeks as guests of Lord and Lady Strathloch and the Honorable Olivia Robertson, who founded the internationally respected society of the Fellowship of Isis. It was in the depths of this castle that my wife, Audrey, was initiated into the hidden Egyptian mysteries of Black Isis by Derry (Lord Strathloch) and Olivia, together with a wonderful woman named Grainne, who was ordained as a priestess of Isis that same day as well. This celebration was followed by an agape (ritual) attended by local occultists, witches, Isians, and a number of eminent Druids.

Each morning, we came together for breakfast and talked about where we had been and what we had seen the previous day, and sometimes Olivia would arrange a special outing for us. Sometimes, as happened on this occasion, Olivia and Poppy (Lady Strathloch) would give us a packed lunch and send us off on our own. Our intention had originally been to go trout fishing at a fish farm. Audrey had never attempted trout fishing and was looking forward to the experience. Smiling, Olivia gave us our little parcel of sandwiches and cakes and bade us a great day.

Our Journey

En route, we accidentally took a wrong turn and found ourselves traveling toward a distant mountain range, so we decided to push on, abandoning the idea of going to the fishery. We had no rods and tackle with us anyway, and we were uncertain of whether we would be able to rent them at the trout farm. Deciding that the mountains looked far more exciting than fishing, we changed our plans. Later we stopped at a small kiosk for a couple of bottles of lemonade, and soon afterward we found ourselves at the base of the mountain. The road up was narrow and tortuous, often with a sheer drop to the side. Indeed, driving along it was a hazardous undertaking in itself!

The drive seemed endless, and we felt as though we were entering into the heavens. Above us, low clouds enveloped the summit. Then, near the apex and to our right, we saw a beautiful valley beneath us; while to our left, a small waterfall cascaded into the depths below. We decided to explore the valley and enjoy our picnic there. It was wild and rugged country, but we succeeded in parking our car in a wider area nearby that would allow another car to pass. Climbing over a fence, we could see the overgrown vestiges of a small path, and so we slowly worked our way down.

After what seemed an eternity, we were able to see the valley more clearly, and at the bottom of it, away from where the waterfall entered a pool, a winding stream wound its way through the valley and disappeared into the distance. A somewhat rickety footbridge now came into sight, and we gingerly made our way down to it. The bridge was clearly disused and rotten, and it was with some trepidation that we made our way across it, with our sandwiches and bottles of lemonade stuck in our pockets. We estimated the stream to be no more than a foot or so deep, so if we did end up in the drink, at least we wouldn't have to swim! Safely across the stream, we wended our way to a spot where harebell and lady's glove were growing and where clumps of bluebell leaves could be seen. The stream tinkled away beneath our feet, and we could hear the sound of the waterfall in the distance. It was an idyllic setting.

Fairy Music

We sat a while, eating our food and drinking lemonade straight from the bottle, but within a few minutes we became aware of a small rustling sound coming from the grass. Audrey is afraid of snakes, so she asked me to investigate, but there was nothing there. Only afterward did it dawn on me that it would have been a fruitless search, as there are no snakes in Ireland—legend states that they were banished by St. Patrick, no less!

The rustling continued circling around us. As the sound suddenly stopped, ever so gently the strains of some kind of ancient music could be heard. It is impossible to describe the ethereal sound that came from the grassy bank. I can only liken it to 11th-century-style music with harpsichords, lutes, and cymbals; it had a distinct medieval air to it, not unlike the sound of the music to the old Tudor song "Greensleeves."

Our first reaction was to look around for overhead wires or telegraph poles, which, just conceivably, could make a kind of singing sound, but the horizon was clear. The clouds had lifted, and all we could see were rolling meadows and hills. We stayed there at least a full half hour before moving on, all the time being serenaded by this mini-orchestra that continuously circumnavigated us. We both noted that this circling around us was "deosil" (counterclockwise), which, we realized when we looked back on the incident, could well have been a significant factor.

It was an absolutely charming scenario, something completely out of this world. The music continued, yet nothing could be seen. We placed our nearly empty bottles in the paper bag and hid them out of sight, intending to return later and retrieve them, and then together we set off to explore the valley. As we walked, the mini-orchestra fell in behind us and followed, dogging our footsteps. Every now and again, the rhythm altered, so that at one point, the music was to our left, then our right, and suddenly in front, as if leading the way. Dutifully we followed, like the entranced children following the Pied Piper of Hamelin. We climbed over turnstiles and five-bar gates and through old overgrown paths, with the merry band traveling along with us, until we stopped and rested for a while.

We sat on the grass, completely puzzled, while the invisible orchestra continued to circle us once more. Eventually we looked at our watches, and as dusk started to fall, we slowly made our way back. Immediately the process started again, with the invisible musicians this time preceding us. Arriving back at the picnic spot, we drank the last vestiges of our lemonade and set off to the car, carrying the now empty bottles with us. To our surprise, the music trailed us right up to the bridge, and as we carefully traversed our way back over it, our tiny minstrels still followed us. The journey back up the hill took far longer than we thought—after all, going downhill is always easier than going up.

Slowly we climbed back up, and all the time, just behind us, the haunting music continued. At long last we came to the car, and right up to the moment we opened the car door, we were regaled with this ethereal music. Then, ever so slowly, as if having seen us safely back to our car, the music receded into the distance. Growing ever fainter, it descended back down into the valley and into the distance until eventually we could hear it no more.

Silently, we started the engine and made our way back down the mountain, wondering about the reality of what had occurred. We pondered the possibilities. We have never owned a portable radio, and at that time we didn't even have a radio in the car. There were no electric lines or telegraph poles in the area (and subsequent inquiries confirmed this). We were in a wild, untamed area that was part of rural Ireland.

Confirmation

The next morning, we joined Derry, Poppy, and Olivia for breakfast, and as usual they inquired as to whether our day had gone well. Derry, a fish lover, asked whether we had caught any fish, but we explained that we had lost our way and ended up on top of a mountain and had picnicked there. Then Derry asked curiously which mountain we were on, at which point we produced our road map and pointed it out.

Our three companions were strangely silent as we pointed out the road we had taken. We then told them of the little valley and of the unsafe old bridge we had chanced crossing. By this point you could have cut the tension in the room with a knife. Then Olivia gently asked, "Did anything happen while you were there?" Reluctant that we may be disbelieved, we started to recall the events of the day, including a description of the valley, the rustic bridge, and the waterfall. They listened in silence, occasionally throwing knowing glances at each other while we described the phenomenon of the magical music we had heard. When we finished our strange story, all three burst into cries of joy, exclaiming that this was wonderful news. They then said how great it was that the valley and its occupants had clearly accepted us and taken us to their bosom.

Local people called the area "the valley of the *sidhe*" (pronounced *shee*). Our friends told us that an occurrence such as ours was very unusual and that no one ever entered the valley for fear of disturbing the "wee ones," or "the little folk." Derry explained that the rows of willow trees that lined the banks of the stream were sacred trees in fairy lore, and apparently spots where willow trees abounded and water tinkled were the most likely places to find fairies. Ponds, lakesides, and riverbanks were also well known fairy haunts, as that was where the little ones often went when they left their burrows. They told us that people had seen fairies beside great oaks and sitting in the branches of rowan and yew trees, all of which were considered magical trees. They also told us that the locals had often heard music in the area around the waterfall that they described as "not of this world" and that the local folk kept away from the area.

When later we went to the shops in the nearby village, we discovered that the story of our encounter had become widely known, and weirdly, no one was surprised at all. The villagefolk knew the place to be a fairy hideaway, and the only thing that surprised them was the fact that we had emerged at least outwardly unaffected. They said that those who heard the music either became enchanted and were lured into the world of fairy and never seen again, or might be replaced by a changeling. Looking back, I wonder whether they really did accept that we were the same people who had arrived earlier.

That evening, Derry opened a bottle of fine wine to celebrate our fairy acceptance. The event became a talking point over the coming weeks, as Derry regaled us with stories of the Tuatha de Danaan, as the little people were known, or the *daoine sidhe*. They were the legendary children of Danu, who were also sometimes called Dana's children. To this day, many an initiated witch will take a fairy name as the name that the coven will thenceforth know her by, and Dana ranks high on the witchcraft list of names.

Legend says these Danaan once ruled Ireland, but then Ireland was invaded by a race known as the Milesians, who overcame the Danaan. Whether these invaders were human is not recorded, but one must assume that they were both human and presumably Christian, for the Danaan fairies were driven underground. At this point in history, the Danaan took up residence in ancient tumuli and barrows, but from within these ethereal chambers they still influenced the lives of the locals—even to this day. (It is interesting to note that J. R. R. Tolkien, who was a great investigator of mysteries such as these, chose to house his hobbits underground!)

The fairies are revered in that part of Ireland, and this devotion is encapsulated in many little customs, such as always leaving a little fruit on the trees at harvesttime for the honored little ones. Another local belief is that farmers must always gather in the corn

The Danaan fairies took up residence in underground burrows

and wheat before November 1, as it would spoil after that day, and fairies hate to see waste.

The following week, Audrey and I left the castle for just a couple of days to stay with the well-known witches Stewart and Janet Farrar. They took us, together with one of their acolytes, named Ginny, to a number of old fairy sites. This journey culminated in a visit to the mystical New Grange. According to local legend, a phantom troupe of ghostly horsemen was known to ride into its interior each full moon. Stewart regaled us with tales of fairy sightings and villagers' experiences relating to the *sidhe*. That night we were awakened by something knocking on the window, and I sleepily got out of bed to see who it was, only to realize that we were sleeping on the top floor of the building and well out of reach of any human. I peered out the window; then, in great excitement, I called Audrey over. There, flapping its wings against the windowpane, was a large bat! It remained there for quite a while, then turned and flew off silently back into the night.

The whole of our five-week stay in Ireland was filled with phenomena, most of it centered on the castle, which I swear was one of the most haunted I have ever stayed in. I would love to devote a chapter in this book to the castle and its apparitions, including the beautiful "girl on the gate," who combed her tresses and sang, and the phantom monks who traversed the old yew walk. However, this book is devoted to fairies and their kin, and strangely enough, fairies were absent from the castle and its immediate precincts.

It has since been suggested to me that we could have been victims of a fairy prank. Apparently, some fairy tribes love to play tricks with strangers, particularly priests; although I was assured that these tricks were normally reserved for Christian ones and certainly not pagan priests like Audrey and me! The Irish people told us that corrigans inhabited some valleys, and these creatures were renowned for their sweet music, which was frequently combined with trickery. They love to lure strangers on a dance, and when I look back, that is exactly what happened, as we were led on a merry dance "up hill and down dale," so to speak, while we followed the music. Corrigans are reputed to reside around streams and ponds, so this legend seems to tally with our experience. They are said to have a particular affection for waterfalls, unlike their fairy cousins, who live in barrows.

Early the following morning, we bade the Farrars a sad goodbye and drove to Ardmore, then back to Huntingdon Castle the following day with our heads full of fairy tales and legends. Sadly, it was the last time I ever saw Stewart, as he passed to the "Summerlands" some time later. Now, years later, as I put pen to paper to write this book, it is still a source of wonderment to both Audrey and me as we recall a sunny day in a sacred valley where none of the locals ventured. We know for a fact that fairies exist, and they are an integral part of our history.

The Art,
Appearance, and
History of
Fairies

2

We who are old, old and gay, O so old!
Thousands of years, thousands of years, If all were told.

—WILLIAM BUTLER YEATS

In distinguishing between fact and fiction and differentiating between popular myth and legend with regard to fairies, we need to abandon the popular idea of what a fairy looks like. Regretfully, the greatest stumbling block in discussing the fairy issue is the popular image of a fairy that was created by our Victorian forebears. They were so entranced by fairies they created the fairy myth that produced the popular image of this ethereal creature that lasts to this day.

The Victorians

Victorian artists illustrated everything from children's books to ornamental cards with beautiful nymphlike young maidens with gossamer butterfly wings in scintillating colors. These figures were clothed in flowing, feminine dresses. Suddenly strict Victorian fathers became keen to read fairy stories to their young broods! A sprinkling of male fairies, usually dressed in little green suits and wearing pointed caps, balance the equation, but the female of the species dominated throughout. The very pretty—and somewhat sexy—image of the fairy entered European consciousness during the 19th century and has remained there right up to the present day.

The trend for pretty fairies started very early on, which shows how deeply fairies were entrenched in history throughout the Western world. Copious works of Ovid refer to them. Shakespeare adored fairies, and when he wrote his famous *A Midsummer Night's Dream*, he catapulted the fairy of yesteryear into a new era. Shakespeare clearly had based his play on an earlier work

The classic Victorian era fairy. *The Spirit of the Night*, 1879, by John Atkinson Grimshaw

entitled *Endimion* by John Lyly. An examination of both plays reveals that there are far too many similarities for this association to be ignored and also shows that there are strong connections to witchcraft and pagan practices in the works. It seems to be a historical fact that, at least until the reign of Elizabeth I, fairies were looked on as naturally as the birds in the air. According to ordinary people, right up to the time of the Tudors, fairies existed—and that was that!

Titania Sleeping in the Moonlight Protected by Her Fairies, by John Simmons (1823–1876)

Research of accounts of sightings and studies of fairies, strangely enough, indicates that the best works were written down by church ministers. In the 1700s, a Sussex vicar wrote the following piece, and we can deduce from his nonchalant tone that fairies were as much a part of nature as were bees and newts!

How lovely it is to see the sun beaming its warmth in the morning, there are toads and frogs in the ponds, the birds are nesting in the trees, the fairies have emerged from their burrows and mounds, and there are primroses and blue-bells in the hedgerows t'is clear that spring is here.

In earlier works, I referred to the fact that the church had never persecuted fairies or issued diatribes against them. In records of courts trials, there are numerous references to situations where reports of a defendant cavorting or associating with fairies were thrown out of court for being irrelevant to the case. (I record some of these in chapter 7.) Further research shows that I was wrong, because it appeared that the church resented fairies, but other than the odd diatribe from the pulpit, ministers tended to criticize rather than condemn them. It appears that fairies were considered an integral part of nature and that people had to tolerate them. In the 1800s, the main target of church disapproval was elves, along with gypsies!

Sex and the Fairies

Many of Ovid's references to fairies were overly sexual, but art-ists used fairies' sexuality to the full. Paintings by the likes of Tintoretto, Titian, Robert Huskisson, and Henry Fuseli were an early form of artistic eroticism. It started with beautiful unadorned females being depicted in fairylike surroundings with Puck, satyrs, fawns, and pards, often in the company of leering elves and goblins. These images graduated into depictions of fairies with wings sitting on toadstools and mushrooms. As time passed, the depictions of fungi became more like phallic symbols, with beautiful nymphets sitting astride them in provocative poses. The sexual symbolism was obvious, and paintings of fairies in this erotic art form became much sought after. Heatherley painted a highly erotic nude sitting on a toadstool with distinctive phalluslike

mushrooms around her, including the one upon which she is sitting. This nude appears to be human because she is wingless, but in the background naked fairies are suspended in the air. Around the central figure a series of phallic toadstools stand out provocatively. This painting is aptly described as "a fantasy."

John Anster Fitzgerald brought a new dimension to this art form, combining fully dressed fairy folk with silent dwarves who viewed these fairy maidens from afar. With the passage of time, Fitzgerald's fairies became more sexual, his portrayals of them more like today's glamorous fashion photographs. In 1867, John Simmons portrayed Titania, the fairy queen from *A Midsummer Night's Dream*, naked with gossamer wings in a woodland setting. This image was probably the most beautiful and erotic fairy ever depicted. A later painting of Titania floating through the air runs a close second. In this painting, she is floating through space, and her wings have been omitted to allow greater emphasis to be paid to her figure.

Children's books now became less sexual and more suitable for their audience, while depictions of the nature of the fairy became more mischievous. This is not surprising, as real fairies are reputed to be full of mischief and always ready to have a laugh at the expense of humankind.

Part Two

FAIRY LORE

The Cottingley Mystery

3

One famous event that fooled even the famous Sir Arthur Conan Doyle, author of the Sherlock Holmes stories, was the mystery of the Cottingley fairies. As a young man, Conan Doyle had studied medicine and surgery, and while he may not have been the father of forensic science, he definitely brought the idea of forensic science and scientific deduction to the notice of the public. However, it seems that he was not an expert in trick photography.

Two cousins, Frances Griffiths and Elsie Wright, who lived in Bradford in the north of England, supposedly photographed the Cottingley fairies. The images were publicized in the *Strand* magazine in 1920, along with an article by Sir Arthur Conan Doyle. The magazine then gave the two girls two dozen photographic plates with which to take more photos. Most of the images the girls took using these plates were useless; the girls blamed the poor outcome on bad weather, despite the fact that the weather had been very good that summer. However, Elsie and Frances came up with a few more fairy images, including one picture of a gnome dressed in clothes from an earlier historical period. Conan Doyle swallowed the evidence whole, believing thoroughly in the fairy photographs, as did many other people, including many magazine and newspaper editors.

In their statements at the time, the two young cousins said that they had discovered the fairies living near a brook and had asked their parents to come and see for themselves. Their parents had simply patronized them and had steadfastly refused to go and see. In frustration, the girls borrowed a camera from Elsie's father, and together they photographed the inhabitants of the fairy colony in order to prove to their families that they were

The illustration from *Princess Mary's Gift Book* (London, 1914), by Claude A. Shepperdson, from which the Wrights girls purportedly created their faked photograph.

telling the truth. A series of circumstances led to the publication of the developed photographs, which stunned the civilized world.

Controversy raged as to whether they could possibly be genuine, but many people felt that they must be, since such young girls would not have the ability to fake the photographs. When the famous Sir Arthur Conan Doyle endorsed the images, the die was cast, and overnight the Cottingley fairies were the new cause célèbre. For many, fairies became an accepted fact, and the fairies, along with the two young girls, were launched across the national press. It was years later when the cousins confessed that the images, created by Claude A. Shepperson, had been cut from a book called *Princess Mary's Gift Book*.

One thing about the Cottingley mystery puzzles me still: While the girls confessed to *some* faking, they didn't confess to it all. When they decided to confess, why didn't they make a clean breast of it, and say that they had never seen any fairies at all? But no! They confessed to faking the pictures, but they never said they hadn't seen the fairies at all.

I have studied the case in detail and have reached the conclusion that Elsie and Frances did genuinely see these ethereal little spirits known as fairies. So why the deception? Perhaps it was in a fit of desperation, after being disbelieved and ridiculed and after trying many times to get their parents to come and see the fairies for themselves, that they faked the photographs simply to prove their point.

Another nagging doubt perseveres: Why didn't the girls photograph the real fairies? Several answers seem to present themselves:

1. Elsie and Frances did try to photograph the fairies, but the little folk did not appear on film because they are ethereal spirits rather than solid flesh.

2. The fairies objected to being photographed, as this would have drawn the attention of adults to their home near the creek.

3. It seems that children, in their innocence, are acceptable to fairies, but adults are not, so the fairies would appear only to youngsters such as the cousins but not to their parents.

4. The fairies found ways of making the girls' parents and other adults keep away from the brook.

This last possibility could provide the answer to another intriguing question: why did neither Conan Doyle nor any member of the press ever try to authenticate the girls' story and visit the site in person? Finally, if the whole thing was nothing more than a fake, why would the story persist until the present day? It is strange, but I have found time and again instances in which people have refused to visit fairy sites or make a real effort to prove or disprove the facts presented to them about the presence of fairies in their midst.

In Later Life

When the cousins were old and near death, they admitted to faking all but one of the photographs. They always maintained that the photo of fairies in a sunbath was genuine. They also held fast to the claim that the fairies had appeared to them near the brook on several occasions. This makes sense in a way. Let us suppose that the fairies became used to seeing the girls and came to trust them; then the girls took a photograph of them. After being caught once in this way, perhaps the fairies prevented the girls from taking any subsequent images. This would have left the girls no option other than to fake the remaining photos. Lastly, the girls were very lucky to get away with cutting up a book, if they did indeed get away with it. Books were expensive, and children were usually punished for drawing on them—the girls' parents would have gone into orbit if they had known that they were cutting up a book!

A Related Mystery

To digress from the Cottingley mystery: There was a highly volatile trial in the 1600s that involved the supernatural. During this trial, the judge, jury, prosecutors, and all the legal experts present in the courtroom were invited to test some evidence and to see for themselves the truth of a particular matter. The man on trial had a whole raft of accusations leveled against him, centering mostly on fairies and witchcraft. The man was reputed to be a great healer, and he maintained that the fairies had trained him. He said that he possessed a highly potent magical powder that he regularly

obtained from the fairy knoll deep in the woods. His defense lawyer demanded that the people in court accompany him to visit the magical glade and see for themselves the truth of the matter. It seems that the experts unanimously decided against accepting the invitation, preferring to acquit the man on all charges instead! Did the fairies keep the crowds away, or were the people too frightened to visit them? Yet another strange mystery . . .

That covers the fairy in history to a certain extent, but in the next chapter let us throw away the Victorian imagery and analyze the fairy to see what it might really have looked like. Truth is sometimes stranger than fiction . . . as you will see.

Encounters of the Fairy Kind

4

Upon a time, before the faery broods
Drove Nymph and Satyr from the prosperous woods,
Before King Oberon's bright diadem,
Sceptre, and mantle, clasped with dewy gem,
Frighted away the Dryads and the Fawns.

—JOHN KEATS, *LAMIA*

That strange and inexplicable encounter in a remote valley in county Wexford in Ireland that I have told you about certainly changed my life. Before that event, I would never have admitted to believing in fairies for fear of ridicule, but the experience that Audrey and I had was real. Furthermore, many other people in that area ratified it. This experience altered my whole outlook on fairy sightings and phenomena.

In England, people look askance at you and regard you as a bit odd if you confess to believing in fairies, but I found quite the reverse in Ireland, where you were regarded as a bit strange if you did *not* believe in fairies! Fairies, or the *sidhe*, as they are known, are part of the Irish heritage, and you have only to bring up the subject in a rural pub on the Emerald Isle to be immediately regaled with tales of encounters with the wee folk.

Derry, Poppy, and Olivia had seen fairies in glades over the years, so they did not hesitate to affirm this phenomenon. They told us that the fairy folk dwelt beneath old burial mounds and ancient tumuli, and that these raised earthworks were called by a variety of names, including the following:

- Other world

- Dragon hills

- The hills of fairy

- Fairy hill

- The hollow hills

The volume of names by which the fairy folk are referred to is endless. These include:

- The barrow people—the name comes from the old tumuli or barrows

- The wee folk

- The hidden ones

- The little people

- The good people

- Mother's blessing

- Our good neighbors

- The people of the hollow hills

- The magical people

- The old people

- The silent people

- The green children

- The fair folk

- Most reverently of all, many refer to them simply as the gentry

Some say that fairies are fallen angels, and a favorite story is that fairies were woodland spirits who were too naughty and mischievous to be allowed into Heaven, as they would cause havoc there. Certainly they have always been notorious for mischief and pranks; however, they were too good to go to Hell.

These little beings are said to be responsible for all the things that mysteriously happen in the human home, such as objects like keys and jewels that go missing and then suddenly reappear

again as if by magic. Some psychics call these events "apports" because things are mysteriously apported to some other spot and, sometimes just as mysteriously, returned. Oh, have we all not suffered at these cunning little hands and wondered just how the missing object has magically reappeared right afterward? Interestingly, when I questioned people about unnatural and inexplicable happenings around their houses, more than 90 percent said they had experienced such things.

It seems that a parallel world once existed alongside our own, a world in which sickness and suffering were unknown, a mysterious realm into which many mortals vanished, never to be seen again, while others went in and reemerged with arcane knowledge that they used for the benefit of humanity. Here a human could spend but a few minutes, only to find countless years had passed in the human realm. In Tír Na nóg, the pixie and fairy world of Otherwhere, time did not exist, or, more precisely, it simply stood still. Well, perhaps even Einstein would agree with that, as when we travel far and fast from the reality of earth, time does indeed slow down.

This parallel world, the realm of fairy, is said to exist beneath tumuli, which are also known as "womb tombs." Legends abound that someday in the future, the fairies will emerge from their hidden kingdom to lead the world to a rebirth of all the old ways.

Irish Fairies

In the here and now, Irish people advise that it is best not to speak to fairies or acknowledge that you can see them, particularly if they are helping you. Later on, you can leave little libations of milk or sweetmeats, especially cream and honey; the fairies will accept these gifts, though they still will not acknowledge you directly.

Members of Irish covens (which are often referred to as Pook covens) implicitly believe in fairies. In many cases, these witches hold their outdoor meetings either on what they describe as "active" fairy rings or on deserted and dormant fairy rings, which can be found everywhere in southern Ireland. Pine forests were rich in these rings, because the tiny mushroom spores from which these rings originated found the soil around pine trees—and around the sacred oak—an ideal nursery.

Country folk knew when the fairies had danced and had a midnight feast, as a fairy circle would appear literally overnight, or they would come across a perfect circle of toadstools that had not been there the day before. These rings are caused by a specific strain of toadstool spore, and they can appear after a heavy dew. A little country poem referred to these and runs as follows:

> If you see a fairy ring
> In a field of grass,
> Very lightly step around,
> And tiptoe as you pass.
> Last night the fairies frolicked there,
> And they're sleeping somewhere near,
> So if you see a tiny fairy,

Lying fast asleep,
Then shut your eyes and run away,
And do not stay to peek.
And never, never, ever tell,
Or else you'll break the fairy spell!

These secretive, fairy-loving Pook covens hold their Sabbats in woodland glades that are steeped in legends of fairy phenomena. Many a coven works where the fairies dwell or have dwelt. Witches have an affinity for fairies, and the witch and fairy communities have protected each other since the beginning of time.

Although these Pook covens are extremely secretive with regard to their activities, my investigations into fairy lore in Ireland and my interviews with those of the Pookarian persuasion have shown me that their sincerity is loud and clear. Woodland fairies are an integral part of their beliefs, and the covens respect them. In fact, some rituals were based on known fairy practices.

Invoking Fairies

It has become clear to me that one does not just happen upon fairies, but that one has to invoke them. The method requires much meditation and some of the gentlest rituals I have ever come across. This process is extremely time-consuming, for if you intend to see fairies, you must be prepared to spend many hours coaxing them to appear, while convincing them of your sincerity.

An old spell that is alleged to conjure up fairies and allows the caster to see into their secret land runs as follows:

Sit where thy cat sits—then cross thy toes.
Close thy eyes and smell a crimson rose.
Then 'neath thy breath—known but to you—
Repeat these words of old, so true.
I believe in fairies, sure as death.
Gadflykin, Gladtrypins,
Come ye Gutterpuss, come ye Cass.
Come to me fairly, both laddie and lass.

Fairy Likes and Dislikes

It was said that another way to conjure fairies was to send a young virgin maiden out the day before a full moon to find a four-leaf clover. Having found the four-leaf clover, the maiden would spend the rest of the day until nightfall making herself a garland of clover (sacred to all fairies) interwoven with myrtle. Then, as evening closed in, she would place the four-leaf clover in her left shoe. Wearing the magic garland on her brow, she would set out to the fairy glen. Seeing her approach, the fairies would appear and welcome her, and she would grow up under their protection, become a healer or wise woman, and have a happy marriage.

Note: Some traditions say that fairies dislike four-leaf clovers and that it is as well to have one or two around to protect oneself from fairy mischief.

When the maiden arrived home, she would scatter foxglove seeds around her front door and plant primroses nearby. She would know that she must never allow the primroses to wither or be neglected, as this would offend the barrow people. They may well have presented her with young primrose roots to plant on her return. Foxgloves that died at the end of the year would be dried and hung above the door as a symbol of welcome.

It appears that roses were very special to fairies, and many old spells and rituals refer to the sweet smell of the rose. Roses of all hues were planted to encourage fairies, but the main essential was scent. Fairies were also enticed by specific libations and gifts of natural foods, plus a final gift of something shiny or glittering. All the people I spoke to while I was gathering evidence for this book told me exactly the same stories.

Country folk would always carry a small sealed flagon of fresh milk or cream with them if they were going anywhere near a fairy stone, a megalith, or sarsen stones, and when they passed the magical spot, they would pour a libation of milk over it. Some people believe that the phrase "Don't cry over spilt milk" comes from the fact that an accidental milk spill was considered a gift for the fairies. In this way, your misfortune at spilling it would actually be a blessing.

In my research, I found that many people, such as Wiccans, locals, farmers, and even the constabulary, provided the strongest evidence of the continued existence of fairies. However, the feeling generally expressed is that, while they still exist, fairies have become what we would now call an endangered species. Crazy as it may seem, fairies seem to be yet another casualty of the population explosion that has taken over the wild places for farming or living space. Everything I have discovered about fairies indicates that they hate to see land ruined by pollution, so perhaps they have disappeared underground or vanished altogether in most places.

One fact that everyone seems to agree on is that the fairies they have seen are nothing like those described in children's books. I must also mention that those who have told me about the fairies they have seen all made me promise not to describe them in detail. What I can do here is record ancient depictions and descriptions of fairies that are in the public domain.

These beliefs were particularly strong in the West Country of England, where belief in the people of the hollow hills was nigh on as fervent as it was among their counterparts in Ireland. Cornish miners working in the tin mines deep underground respected the troglodyte denizens whom they were likely to encounter while working there. If the miners lost or mislaid a shovel or pick, the barrow people would find it for them and leave it nearby to be discovered later. No Cornishman would ever make the sign of the cross while toiling underground for fear of offending the little spirits who watched over him and his colleagues.

The first thing that strikes one when reading old reports of fairy sightings is the high intelligence level of these elusive little denizens of the diva kingdom. They are described as cigar-shaped, globular, and spherical. These creatures are also universally depicted as translucent, with wings and dark mellow eyes. They both hover and flit, and are extremely curious, always examining, yet warily keeping their distance. This description

seems to link with UFO sightings and events, so perhaps these are one and the same.

It is known that fairies frequent woodland glades and shady areas that are full of fallen trees, rotting logs, and emerald mosses. They are seen around ponds, where they flit alongside the dragonfly, lacewing, mayfly, and firefly. They visit these gathering places from grassy mounds beneath which the fairies have burrowed out tunnels to establish one of their colonies. Apparently, though, the majority of these colonies are to be found beneath old tumuli and burial chambers.

From around most of the barrows, or tumuli, in areas around Cork, the local museums have collected a number of so-called elf bolts, which are allegedly the tips of elves' arrows. The elves would shoot these weapons at intruders or at those who had offended them. Of course, this is just legend, for we now know that these are Neolithic arrowheads used by our ancestors for hunting. Most of these arrowheads have been brought to the surface by rabbits burrowing into the old Neolithic burial chambers. But fact, fantasy, magic, mystery, and reality mix together, and after all, it was beneath these ancient tumuli, among these dead ancestors of ours, that the fairies set up their colonies.

To this day, farmers in Ireland always plow around these tumuli. The law states that they must give them a wide margin, but the farmers give them an even wider one than the law suggests. It appears that their fathers and grandfathers always respected the hollow hills and would not intrude on the little ones. In fact, they would not plow up the fairy rings or erect barns or dwellings on or near a fairy path. Old customs die hard, even in our century, and there are places even now where local people protested against a development in an area where a fairy kingdom was supposed to be active. They saved the area from the bulldozers.

Finding Fairies

5

f you want to try your hand at seeing fairies, you need to get out into the countryside. Tradition says that the best place to see them is in a wood and near water, but while this is fine in Europe and some parts of North America, not everyplace has woods and streams. Wherever you live, your best bet is to get as far from human habitation as you can. It is said that fairies hate pollution and mess, and there may be something to that, as they tend to avoid places where humans rush around working and shopping. However, the evidence that I have picked up while writing this book shows that fairies don't necessarily move too far from human habitation either. For instance, a friend of mine once saw a fairy in a small wood in a part of north London that is called Harrow-on-the-Hill. The area that the fairy lived in was not very far from the grounds of Harrow School, where Winston Churchill and many other eminent men were once educated. It appeared that the noise of boys playing cricket and rugby football didn't put the fairies off living in that area.

The Method

Your best bet is to search out a quiet place where you can meditate in peace. You will need to find a tree that you can sit down by or, failing that, a rock. You will need to lean back and have as much of your body as possible in touch with the tree or rock.

Now dig out all those crystals and tumbled rocks that you have bought over the years and then left to gather dust in the closet. Give them a good wash. If you can, gather rainwater and wash them in that, and then leave them out to dry. If you have to wash the crystals in tap water, do so, but then leave them in clean cold water with a little salt for an hour or two. When this is done, spread them out on a cloth and let them dry naturally. If you can leave them outdoors at night when the moon is full or approaching full, so much the better. When you have prepared the crystals and tumbled stones, put them in a clean bag.

You will need to take a gift along with you—a little honey, some small cakes, or some milk or cream. You might take a pretty little bowl, a small cup, or even a pretty eggcup with you, but do ensure that it is one you are prepared to live without, as you will need to leave it behind for the fairies when you come away. Alternatively, you might place some cakes on a leaf or make a little dish out of some biodegradable material such as wood.

You will also need to take something along that you feel gives you a measure of protection—a pentacle, a religious talisman, or some other amulet, perhaps even a favorite teddy bear. You will bring this home with you once you have finished, so you can take something that is meaningful to you. I would avoid taking shiny objects, jewelry, or any valuable that has a sentimental value, as this type of thing has a habit of disappearing when fairies and elves are around! Don't forget to take some water to drink and perhaps a piece of fruit or some dried fruit and nuts to keep you going.

Once you get to your chosen spot, lay the crystals and stones in a large circle or oval shape around the tree or rock, and leave enough room for you to sit within the crystal enclosure.

Now sit inside the circle and open your chakras. Chakras are psychic centers in the body that, once open, allow you to reach levels of consciousness that would otherwise not be accessible to you.

Opening the Chakras

The word "chakra" is a Hindu word that means "wheel." There are seventy-eight thousand chakras spread around the body, but we need concern ourselves with only seven of them. Five of the chakras go through the body from front to back at specific points along the spine, while the sixth is in the center of the forehead and the last is on the crown of the head.

Before you consider opening the chakras, ask your spiritual guides or angels for protection, as you might leave yourself open to something that you would rather not attract. Use this short prayer for protection:

Act like a charm
To protect me from all harm
While my senses awake
And this journey I take

Say this little prayer three times, as that will increase its power. Then say "So be it."

The colors of the chakras are the same as the colors in a rainbow:

- The crown chakra is purple
- The forehead chakra (or third eye) is dark blue
- The throat chakra is light turquoise blue
- The heart chakra (around the breastbone area) is green
- The spleen chakra (the area of the diaphragm) is yellow
- The solar plexus chakra (the middle of the abdomen) is orange
- The base chakra (the base of the spine) is red

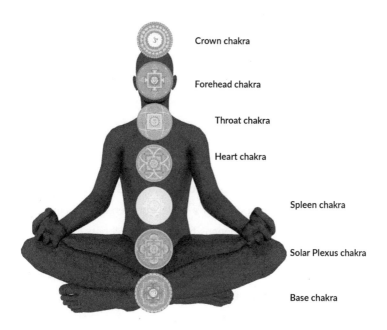

Crown chakra

Forehead chakra

Throat chakra

Heart chakra

Spleen chakra

Solar Plexus chakra

Base chakra

To open the chakras, you must imagine yourself gathering light from the whole universe. Then bring this light down to the crown chakra. See the crown chakra as a purple lotus (water lily) and imagine it opening and allowing the light to enter through it into your head. Then allow the light to come down inside your head and around it as far as the forehead chakra, where a large blue eye opens. Allow the light to come down as far as the throat, where a pale blue flower opens. Allow the light to come down to the heart chakra, where a bunch of green leaves opens. Allow the light to come down to the spleen chakra and let a large yellow daisy or dahlia open. Allow the light to come down to the solar plexus chakra, where a large orange marigold opens. Allow the light to come down to the base chakra, where a big red poppy opens up.

Then allow the light to filter down through your legs and to fill your whole body and the surrounding aura. Finish by imagining the light extending down into the bowels of the earth. Surround yourself and fill yourself with this light, and allow it to contain a little gold, as if it were subtly touched with a little of the precious metal's dust.

A Meditative State

Now relax and allow yourself to get into a kind of meditative state. You can close your eyes for a while, but then open them again, relax, and let what happens happen. You will notice more than you would in a normal state, so you will become more aware of the breeze on your skin, the sound of leaves rustling, or the wind moving through the trees. You will see colors more sharply than usual, and you might start to see something flitting around in the corner of your eye. You may see fairies, angels, elves, something else, or nothing, but you may very well start to see elementals, which are like insects or small animals that don't really exist but whose shadow seems to be flitting around. Elementals are a lucky sign, and if you do see them, you can be sure that good luck will follow within a week or two.

Closing Your Chakras

If nothing happens, or even if you fall asleep for a while, this doesn't matter. It is vitally important to close your chakras once you have finished, however, or you may find yourself "invaded" by bad dreams or other unwanted aftereffects. Simply reverse the opening procedure, turning off the light and closing your chakras one after the other.

Start by imagining the light that has reached down into the earth being turned off. Then turn off the light in your legs until you reach the base chakra. Now turn off the light there and carefully close down the red poppy. Now turn off the light up to and beyond the solar plexus and close that flower down tightly. Continue the process until you have finished, and then send the light off into the universe.

Have a drink of water and eat a little fruit; then gather your things together, leaving the little gift of food, milk, or cream for the fairies, and come back again to repeat the whole process another time. If there are fairies or other elemental creatures in the area, the fact that you left them something nice will encourage them to come near next time around. If nothing happens in that spot after two or three tries, try another spot.

Other Considerations

Don't forget that you might pick up on other supernatural beings, such as elves, pixies, goblins, dwarfs, trolls, and some fairly unpleasant ones as well, so do ensure that you cast your little spell for protection, and you should be safe.

Whether the fairy experiment works or not, you will start to notice other things happening in the days that follow. You might have prophetic dreams, increased psychic awareness, elementals within your home, or just a feeling of being happier and more in control of your life.

- Tradition says that you might expect to see fairies on any day of the week other than Friday or Monday.

- Although modern-day individuals may not like to think of them in this way, tradition states that fairies are guardians of the dead and safeguard the souls of the dead—hence their attraction to barrows and graveyards. This connection provides evidence that good days for fairy spotting are the Thursday before Easter, Easter Sunday itself, and Ascension Day.

- Fairies are also particularly associated with spring, and they are known to enjoy being around spring flowers. In light of this tendency, the connection to the Christian festival of Easter makes sense, as this holiday is associated with death and rebirth in religious terms, and with the rebirth of spring in the Northern Hemisphere. Another especially good day is the vernal equinox, which falls on March 21. Naturally, Halloween and All Souls' Day are notably good times, as is any full moon. However, all reports about fairy activity suggest that you should avoid looking for them or approaching their preferred areas during the hours of darkness, as they can become rattled and then malicious.

- Incidentally, there is a connection between moths and butterflies and fairies, as these insects are also considered to be guardians of the souls of the dead.

- If you find a small hill or a fairy ring, which might be a ring of discolored grass or a ring of toadstools, you must circle it three times "widdershins" (counterclockwise) while calling, "Open door! Open door! And let me come in!"

Look carefully when you see a swarm of butterflies!
(Detail from Richard Doyle, illustration for *In Fairyland*, 1870)

- If you can't get out and about but still want to contact the fairies, try looking at a picture of a fairy and allowing yourself to fall into a meditative state. You might find that you receive a message later that day or at night while you sleep.

- Don't be surprised if, when you come back to reality, you find that time has shrunk or stretched, so that whatever time you think you have spent on the fairy hunt is far shorter or longer than you thought.

Other Entities

These are some of the entities you may encounter on your fairy-finding quest.

Dwarves

By tradition, dwarves are miners, so they have an affinity with those who work down in the mines. Miners say that they like to share a little of their food with the dwarves. Devon miners call their meal "cram," while Cornish miners call theirs "craust." These words have gone into the language of miners as far away as Australia and the United States, and in all places miners like to keep on the right side of the dwarves by giving them a little of their lunch.

Brownies

Brownies are said to be household fairies that help in the home, particularly when there is a baby living there. This suggests that brownies are not susceptible to being hurt or killed by coming into contact with metal, because modern homes are full of metal, and even ancient homes had some metal pots and tools around. If things go missing and then turn up again in your home, you can always blame the brownies for borrowing them.

Gremlins

During World War II, when an airplane wouldn't operate properly or things went missing in the hangar, Royal Air Force pilots and engineers used to say that there were "gremlins" at work. These creatures were completely mythical—but can we be sure of that?

Protection

If you fear that fairies, gremlins, gnomes, goblins, dwarves, brownies, or any other supernatural beings are troubling you, make a charm for yourself out of something green—such as a piece of green paper with a pretty drawing on it or a favorite green button. Keep the green paper or object in your pocket or wear something green on a string around your neck.

Gremlins, as depicted by Francisco Goya in *Los Caprichos*, 1799

A True Modern Fairy Story

6

'Tis merry, 'tis merry, here in Fairy-land,
When fairy birds are singing,
When the court doth ride by their monarch's side,
With bit and bridle ringing:
—SIR WALTER SCOTT, *THE LADY OF THE LAKE*

When I said a modern fairy story, I meant just that, for the scene that is about to unfold took place in the autumn of 2005. A development company had purchased a parcel of land close to Loch Earn, which is near the village of St. Fillans in Perthshire, Scotland. The area was famous locally for the crystal streams that flowed down the mountainsides, from which the local people made whisky. The people of the nearby villages are godly folk, but in this rural area, one pagan belief still prevails, and that is the locals' belief in the world of fairy!

The development company went through all the normal procedures in applying for building permission, and the local council gave its stamp of approval as to how many houses could be built there. Thus, with all his documents now in order, the developer set about laying the foundation for his new project. Little did the developer and council know that somewhere deep in the caverns in the center of the site there was a stirring, as news of the impending development reached the realms of fairy. It is said that hundreds of little telepathic messages went out to the many sympathizers around the little colony, imploring their help.

At the break of day one morning some time later, the heavy clunking of the bulldozers was heard as they made their way onto the potential development, shaking the ground in the center like a subterranean earthquake. Slowly the great machines moved in on their first target: a massive stone in the center of the site. This stone was as old as time itself, and it was steeped in history as well. The little ones had dwelt for millennia in safety under the shelter of this gigantic granite protrusion, but now the huge machines edged ever closer to their hallowed land.

With the rock firmly in his sights, the driver started to lower the great shovel. He had been instructed to move the rock intact, to place it by the roadside, and there ornament it with the name of the new development. Sacrilege! And what would replace it? Would some new house eventually cover the home that was the fairy city? Would tons of concrete cement the wee folk into their subterranean chambers? Or would they be able to burrow out, only to find themselves in an area where cars were a daily hazard? As the eleventh hour drew near, a villager who had heard what was about to happen raced to the scene to save the fairy hiding place. He hurled himself in front of the advancing mechanical monster, crying out, "Do not touch that rock! You will kill the fairies!" Little did he know it, but at that moment (if local legend is to be believed) a number of "elf bolts" were undoubtedly aimed at the bulldozer's driver. Apparently, if the bolts had struck home they would have given the bulldozer driver and the other workers dreadful rheumatism. The message here, as ever, is not to meddle with the little ones!

Within hours, the whole project had developed into a standoff, as the locals gathered to defend the fairy colony and adhere to their traditions of never allowing the great standing stone to be moved. Rocks thereabouts were steeped in history and were part of the local heritage, but this rock in particular was covering far more than a colony of fairies. It was said to be like the famous Stone of Scone, where kings were crowned, because this one was a relic of the Pictish kings. (The Picts are an ancient Celtic race that lived in Scotland.) The people petitioned councilors and dug out old deeds and local laws that showed the history of the rock.

Past History

Apparently, in the distant past, Pictish kings traveled to have their crowns placed upon their royal heads on the magical fairy rock, undoubtedly to obtain a fairy blessing and promise of protection at the same time. Here on the hillside where the mountain of Dundurn descended, a Celtic missionary by the name of St. Fillan attempted to convert the pagan Picts to Christianity, but the Picts refused. St. Fillan was naturally somewhat put out by their refusal, but finding heather and gorse to his liking, along with the excellent whisky the people brewed in that area, he decided to settle there. The fairies probably ignored him as long as he did not build a church and start ringing bells. (Legend states that fairies cannot abide church bells. This may be because in medieval and Saxon times, when people started to build a church in an isolated area, it meant that a village would soon grow up around it, thus making the area unsuitable for fairies to live there any longer.)

What Happened Next

The locals scanned historical records, and they put up a fight to "save the fairies!" Of course, the press joined in. The whole village was united, and its inhabitants resolved to save the fairy colony at all costs. The builder seems to have been a reasonable man who was anxious not to upset the villagers, and presumably he was even keener not to upset the fairies. He agreed to redraw the plans, leaving the fairy colony to prosper, after which the Perthshire planning committee decreed that the area was technically in a national park. In the arguments put forth by residents, a statute said that planning law specifically states that "local customs and beliefs must essentially be taken into consideration when any new development was proposed," which means that if the locals believe a place to be inhabited by fairies, it must be treated as such!

The result was a stupendous victory! Fairy magic worked, helped just a little bit by the volume of protest from all at St. Fillans and the national press. Now, as the plans were redrawn, the little fairy colony beneath the ancient stone that had stood since time immemorial was safe, and would be so for future generations. The fairies still ruled the little area around them, and peace was restored to the sleepy village.

So, a fairy story? Yes, but a modern and true one. The little ones must have made merry at the news. They know that each morning there will be little libations of milk and honey put out for them as of old; the local people would keep up old customs by offering the traditional "clouties" (gifts of food); and maybe there would be a little something shiny placed among the gifts once in a while as well. Maybe, just maybe, when nobody is looking, the developer also puts out a little sweetmeat as an offering.

A Magical Scene

7

*Unluckily the Hills are empty now, and all the
People of the Hills are gone. I'm the only one left.
I'm Puck, the oldest Old Thing in England,
very much at your service*

—RUDYARD KIPLING, *PUCK OF POOK'S HILL*

A trial for witchcraft involving fairies took place in Dorset, in England, in 1566. The accused was called John Walsh. There does not seem to be much doubt that he was a witch, and a proficient one at that. Long before he was arrested and arraigned on a charge of practicing witchcraft, he was well known as a healer who was proficient with the knife and scalpel, a rare qualification in those days. I gather from old records that he knew the correct way to cast the magic circle, having been taught the proper technique by his master, Sir Robert Drayton, to whom he had been a manservant for seven years. By the time of the trial, Sir Robert had been dead for several years, so he at least was beyond the law.

Walsh was alleged to have been seen "consorting with fairies." He saw nothing wrong in this, so when he was questioned he readily admitted it. Once again it would appear that, to Walsh at least, the existence of fairies was considered as natural as the presence of birds or bees; they were just a part of nature and accepted as such.

Walsh had no hesitation in answering his interrogators. He gave explicit details of how he approached the fairies and stated that it essentially had to be between noon and one in the afternoon, or else at midnight. This timing links with other contemporary reports, although I could find no evidence of his having given the traditional three knocks in a secret and certain way to summon the fairies, as has been recorded elsewhere. Walsh told the judge and jury the tumulus would then open to admit him. I can only assume he did use some kind of secret knock, for he never disclosed it during the trial, nor was he asked to do so. Amazingly, this evidence and confession were passed over by the judge as "being of no consequence." The judge stated that no one in his right mind doubted the existence of the little folk, as they were a fact of life. Both the prosecutor and the judge were more concerned with the fact that Walsh kept a toad as a familiar, and the judge asked him whether he talked to it!

The reason I quote this trial in particular is because of the casual way the fairies were regarded. For instance, when Walsh referred to one of the "great heaps of earth where the fairies dwell," he nonchalantly offered to prove his point and take judge and legal experts there. The bench decided that it was not necessary, which emphasizes that the existence of fairies was accepted without question. The Walsh case is unique, not only because of the fairy element, but also because Walsh was acquitted of the crime of witchcraft on the grounds of insufficient evidence.

The World of Law

For the record, I mention in passing that I spent eleven years working in the legal field in Britain, specializing in ancient and antiquated laws that were still enforceable in the 20th century. In this capacity, I was often consulted on ancient and remote precedents in law that could still be quoted and enforced, owing to the fact that they had never been repealed. It was in this capacity that I was referred to in legal circles as "the Devil's Advocate." You can therefore imagine my surprise at finding a law, passed in 1153 during the reign of Henry III and still in existence, that made it a capital offense to kill a fairy! (Of course, the death penalty in Great Britain has long since gone out of existence.)

Laws are not passed without reason, and there has to be a large degree of substance before an issue is legislated against, so why were fairies protected? The church was prone to condemn anything that even remotely suggested any form of supernatural or occult activity, but it never turned entirely against fairies. Although they were criticized, never to my knowledge did the church ever outright attack fairies. In all the archives that I have scoured, the closest thing I ever found to an attack was one reference where a churchman described fairies as "Angels expelled from Heaven." Mostly fairies were referred to somewhat benevolently as the "Handmaidens of Nature." But there is no escaping the fact that the existence of fairies was accepted as a solid fact, with the best recordings written by clergymen.

France doesn't seem to have been as fairy friendly: The Maid of Orleans, the legendary Joan of Arc, was charged with witchcraft, as we know, but one of the accusations against her was that "she did consort with fairies and did dance with them." Under torture, Joan confessed that she had seen them flying with friends every Thursday! Despite all the torture, nobody managed to produce a fairy at Joan's trial.

It was not until the 1700s that a campaign commenced chastizing country people for dancing around old burial barrows; offering libations to wee folk, fairies, and elves; or having fairy charms on houses and barns. The church sought to discourage country folk from inviting these little people of the hills to enter human habitations, no matter how benevolent they might be.

One clergyman went as far as preaching to the congregation that he was perturbed at the fact that local children had been seen "cavorting with elves" by the old burial mounds and playing with gypsy children as well. It seems that fairies, goblins, and gypsies were considered part of the same group!

One thing that comes over loud and clear is the rapport that seems to have existed between fairies and local witches. Isobel Halfgane, a Scottish witch, alleged that it was the fairies who taught her magic. To this day, modern witches visit and worship the old gods in the valleys and mounds that were reputed to have been the homes of fairies.

Another witch, Alison Peirson, was said to have consorted with fairies and learned magical healing arts from them as a young girl. She was reputed to be the most advanced healer of her day, and it was not long before news of her healing powers spread throughout the county. This news eventually reached the ears of the archbishop of St. Andrew, who lay dying. The doctors of the day could do nothing to save him and eventually agreed to send for the fairy woman who could perform miracles with her healing powers. Alison took pity on him and applied her secret herbs and potions to him, as taught to her by the fairies. The archbishop, to the surprise of everyone, made a full recovery and was able to return immediately to his ecclesiastical duties. Was he grateful to Alison? Oh, no; to him, the miracle that she had performed was fairy power, combined with the devil's own works and arts. No sooner had the archbishop recovered than Alison was seized and burned at the stake. The stingy old archbishop did not have to pay the meager fee his benefactor had requested!

During the time of the witch hunts, unsurprisingly the wise witches started to disappear. Interestingly, the fairy colonies started to disappear around the same time. Local traveling churchmen made occasional reports on their local fairy colonies, and these make interesting reading due to the casual manner in which the clergy accepted the existence of the colonies, some going as far as to actually study them.

One clergyman's diary from the 1790s reads that he "fears the local fairy colony is dying out." Apparently he made a trip to a remote part of the countryside and commented on the fairies' scarcity. Some years later, in 1796, he reports his sorrow at there being no more than a score of fairies there now, and in the following report, two years later, in 1798, he writes that at his last observation there were but six left. His last report (undated but believed to be 1800 or 1801) states that the colony is no more, and that upon his last visit, in 1800, it was overgrown with bramble and nettles, and that he had not seen a fairy there for more than a year.

Personal Research

In June 2006, my wife and I set off to follow the path that the clergyman had taken. We followed an old route across wild countryside to a remote old house that was listed on the map as "black hole," which itself is an intriguing description. We found a handful of caravans at first, but at the end of the lane there was a gate, and beyond it lay our destination.

Wild, haunted, and awe inspiring was the breathtaking beauty of rolling woods and hills. Yes, this was truly a place where fairies could have lived, and although they were recorded as being extinct, the area was vibrant. As I looked around the tumbling hills, I had the feeling that little minds were saying, "We do exist, and we always have." This was truly fairyland in green and brown, with myriad flowers in scintillating colors abounding in an untamed wilderness. In the distance, there was the faint lowing of cattle, and somewhere far off a horse whinnied. Above us a bright sun sent dappled light filtering through the trees.

We stayed for a while, then started to make our way back down the tortuous track. Did the little folk give us signs as we retreated? How can we tell? There is no proof, but the remarkable events that occurred as we made our way back were so frequent that we had to wonder whether some supernatural forces were at work. The moment we started back, a young raven hopped out of the hedge about twenty yards away and sat there unperturbed as we approached him. When we reached him, our ebony friend casually hopped out of our way to let us pass. We were so close I could have touched him. We continued on our way when we suddenly realized the bird was following us; then he came up to us and stopped by our feet. Audrey's immediate reaction was to think that he was hurt, but when I moved to pick him up, he flew up onto the fence as if to say, "No, I'm not hurt. I'm all right." Then he promptly flew down again in front of

us and led the way like a sentinel, hopping about three feet ahead of us the whole time.

Next, a couple of young fox cubs examined us curiously until we were out of sight. They were completely and utterly unafraid.

Then a giant hare raced toward us. A hare is a truly magical sign in Celtic lore, for the Celts held them to be sacred. In one of her great battles against the Roman army, Boudicca, queen of the Iceni people of eastern England, released a hare before the battle began, for it would show her the path to take and direct her to the weakest area in the enemy's lines. It did, and the Celts vanquished the Romans.

The hare stopped just in front of us, hesitated, and then, standing on his haunches, he stared at us for a while. Then, like the fox cubs, he watched us until we walked past him before he casually loped off. We watched as he headed away from us to our immediate left, and then we suddenly saw two young leverets leap high up into the air on our right.

I have seen hares box and leap before, but this time the leap was truly miraculous, and it riveted our attention. The leverets raced in circles, boxed each other, and, making miraculous leaps, raced toward and then leaped over each other. It was like watching a display of the Red Arrows at an air show. I am a countryman, well used to seeing the antics of hares, and I have seen them leap many times, but the heights that these animals reached were phenomenal. It seemed that while we were walking through the area, we were invisible to the local wildlife!

We made our way home later that evening, having explored the site of the last fairy that was seen in Britain. More than two hundred years had passed since that last sad sighting, but the hills rolled for as far as the eye could see. No vast building developments had taken place in the intervening period; no excavators had leveled the still visible mounds. Here on the hill, time had stood still for more than two centuries, and if the barrow folk did still exist, then undoubtedly this would be the place to find them.

Something Odd

I must mention one last weird thing. The area that Audrey and I were in on that afternoon was in Sussex in southern England, not far from the south coast. The area was called Harrow Hill. The place that my friend Eva sat when she saw her fairies was called Harrow-on-the-Hill!

The name "Harrow" is common and has its roots in farming terminology. Harrow-on-the-Hill is different. The hill rises out of a flat landscape, and there has been a settlement on the hill since the Ice Age. The name "Harrow" is a corruption of the early Iron Age word "herga," which meant hill.

Part Three

ENTERING THE FAIRY REALM

Fairy Mysteries, Flowers, and Charms

8

Over hill, over dale,

Thorough bush, thorough brier, . . .

I do wander everywhere,

Swifter than the moon's sphere;

And I serve the Fairy Queen.

—SHAKESPEARE, *A MIDSUMMER NIGHT'S DREAM*

Clergymen predominate in fairy research, and considering their tendency to condemn anything that has even the remotest connection with the otherworld or the occult, they write about fairies in an amazingly positive manner. One Scottish minister named the Reverend Robert Kirk, who lived in the 1600s, made a highly detailed study of fairies and was regarded as an authority on them. He wrote a book entitled *The Secret Commonwealth of Elves, Fauns, and Fairies*. Regretfully, because of his strange and untimely death, the book was not published until 150 years later. He would observe fairy colonies for hours on end, making copious notes throughout. He ignored locals who continuously warned him against outstaying his welcome at the fairy mound. When he did not come back one day, nobody was surprised, for they all knew that "Robbie had been taken by the fairies."

Halfhearted search parties combed the area for him, knowing they had little chance of success, for they knew he would be deep beneath the ground. When his body was discovered sometime later, at what appears to have been a burial mound or tumulus, it was still widely believed that the corpse discovered was a changeling. The villagers believed that the Reverend Robert Kirk was now learning the magic arts somewhere deep down below. The question of whether he had gone with the fairies voluntarily or not was a hot topic of conversation for a very long time.

At Pulborough Mount in Sussex, local, villagers reported seeing a fairy funeral and they were so concerned that they called in the local vicar to authenticate it. He wrote up this event to confirm what he had seen. The date was 1800, so it appears that even up to this relatively recent time, records suggest that fairies existed in great profusion throughout the country. Only in the 20th century do they seem to die out, notwithstanding the fact that there have been reports of fairy sightings, albeit singly or in small numbers, right up to the present day.

Leslie Philips, a well-known researcher of the paranormal, reported seeing a fairy on Chantonbury Ring on All Hallows Day (Hallowmass) in the late 1960s or early 1970s. Apparently he called up a number of witnesses to verify the sighting.

In the late 1800s, the famous witch woman Biddy Earl, the wise woman of County Clare, was reputed to have received her powers from the fairies, and it is said that they bestowed on her a wondrous elixir in a translucent bottle of light blue glass. Some legends say she won the magical bottle and its elixir in a game of chance when she was gambling with a fairy. (The church said she gambled against the devil.) Whatever the truth of the matter is, we shall never know, because when she died in 1873, locals threw her wonder bottle into a nearby lake, and it was seen no more.

The last official sighting and recording of a fairy colony is at Harrow Hill at Patching in Sussex. So now it appears that the age of fairies is over and the fairies are extinct. Or are they?

Wales and the West Country

Rumors persist as to sightings in Wales and the West Country. The last report that came my way was in 2005, but regretfully this report remains unsubstantiated. There is far too much evidence to dismiss claims of these sightings peremptorily. My experience is that those who testify to such phenomena are invariably quite rational people, so I cannot dismiss their reports out of hand.

Naturally, my whole outlook with regard to the world of fairy altered overnight after that amazing incident in Ireland in 1981. What did happen that day? We had no radio with us, nor did we have one in the car; there were no telegraph poles for miles and no transmitters of any description. But whenever we mentioned the incident locally, people beamed and said, "We know that is where the *sidhe* live; we call them the *daoine sidhe*." This is Irish for "fairy folk;" it is pronounced *theena shee.*

Audrey and I made another discovery on our return to England, and that is the magic that is associated with primroses and fairies.

There is a widespread belief that if you eat primroses you will be able to see the fairy folk, and once upon a time, village children ate the flowers in the hopes of seeing fairies. It would be interesting to note if a primrose contains hallucinogens. We know for a certainty that these plants have healing powers, for in the New Forest, the woodsmen used to concoct ointment of primroses and lard to put on wounds.

On May Day, when witches were supposed to be particularly active, bunches of primroses would be placed on the doorways of barns and cottages to keep them out, but apparently this backfired, because a bunch of dried primroses hung over a doorway is an invitation! There are many superstitions associated with witches, primroses, and fairies; according to one, if you pick these beautiful flowers for a posy, then make sure you pick at least thirteen, because any fewer will invite bad luck.

If you go for a walk in the countryside, you should take a little wooden wand (also known as a *stang*) or twig with you, as this will keep you safe if you inadvertently cross a fairy grove. If you carry such a wand with you to an ancient tumulus and spend the night on it, then the fairies will appear and accept you, and you may even be invited to join in their festivities. (Note: I am not sure I would want to spend the night alone on an ancient burial site with nothing but a bit of wooden wand for protection. Far too spooky!)

If you stand in a fairy ring that is surrounded by toadstools, legend has it that you will become trapped in the circle for a year and a day. You will dance a fairy polka nonstop while you are there. One woman told of how she wandered onto a fairy ring

The fairy ring. (Richard Doyle, from *In Fairy Land*, a series of pictures from the elf-world, 1870)

and danced in this way, but at the end of her time she stayed on and spent the next six years dancing without becoming fatigued, as it was such a joyous experience. Well, it seems that we can't believe everything we hear, can we? Modern people know that a fungus creates fairy rings and that toadstools are also a form of fungus, but I leave it up to you as to whether you want to jump into a fairy ring that is surrounded by toadstools or not.

Myth and Reality

The Scot Thomas the Rhymer was wary of fairies, perhaps because he had some kind of premonition about them. Apparently, he disappeared mysteriously one day, only to reappear some days later a changed man. He said that he had accidentally stepped into a circle of toadstools, only to realize too late that he was in a magical fairy circle. Before he could react, and with his guard down, he was instantly transported to fairyland. He came back with the gift of prophecy, and he became famous as a seer and poet, both skills he said he learned from the fairies. He predicted the death of Alexander III, king of Scotland, and the battle of Bannockburn.

Morgan le Fay was reputed to be a fairy in human form. She spent her whole life among humans, but she had phenomenal magical powers including the ability to fith-fath, or change her shape at will. It is recorded that she used her fairy powers wrongly; therefore, the fairy council declared her persona non grata, and no fairy would speak to her. You can find this story in the legends of King Arthur.

Morgan le Fay, by Edward Burne-Jones, 1862, Leighton House Museum

Apparently fairies like to live among primroses, harebells, foxgloves, lady's gloves, and bluebells. They also are fond of elderberry wine, and it flows as their revels reach fever pitch. Legend says that the fairies would lead little fairy horses adorned with bluebell heads that formed blue collars. According to lore, the wee ones danced in a state of high ecstasy because they had drunk the sap of the foxglove, which they made into a drink by some secret method. These secret practitioners were known as the Tuatha de Danaan, which is Irish for "the Little People of the Goddess." They imbibed their secret potions and then sucked the stamens dry. Legend says that these little ones who pursued this particular practice were the remnants of a near extinct tribe of the descendants of Dana.

Fairies among the flowers. (Richard Doyle, from *In Fairy Land*, a series of pictures from the elf-world, 1870)

Since my experience in Ireland, my whole outlook has altered, and now when I am asked whether I really believe that fairies exist, my answer has to come down on the positive side. Please understand that what I am about to record is purely my own personal opinion, but the evidence of fairy phenomena is overwhelming. We now know that for a thousand years their existence was never doubted and that they are part of our history and part of our heritage.

One witch I know has a house that simply swarms with elementals. They scurry around her floor like hundreds of little black beetles. Be honest and answer truthfully: Have you not seen little dark patches flit across the floor and wondered what they were? Well, undoubtedly this is an elemental or woodland spirit. These are extremely common and are to be welcomed; they are little friendly creatures, and they are little protectors as well, so love them and they will love you in return. Fairies are also elementals that are a part of the mysterious diva kingdom. Sometimes there are little woodland spirits flitting across little glades where wild flowers grow.

Fairy Rings and Superstitions

9

This is Mab, the Mistress Fairy
That doth nightly rob the dairy.

—BEN JONSON

airies are said to dance so much, and for such long periods at a time, that a whole colony of little leprechauns is usually entrenched nearby—so when you find fairies, you will also find leprechauns and pixies. The reason that the leprechauns are so close by is so the fairies do not have to walk far to get new shoes. A fairy's feet will be sore from dancing, and as we all know (well, most of us), leprechauns are the famous shoemakers. They are engaged full-time in manufacturing footwear for elves, pixies, goblins, and so on, but the fairies are always their best customers.

Oberon, Titania, and Puck with Fairies Dancing, William Blake, c. 1786

Fairies in History

Over the years, fairies have been regarded askance by those of the cloth because of their revelry. Alongside gypsy children, who were said to be friendly with the elves, fairies were the subjects of vitriolic outbursts from the pulpit. The clergy tried to dissuade fairies from mixing with elves and gypsies, as when joined together, these groups were considered to be a particularly bad combination of forces. Believe me—I am not making any of this up!

Let us now go back into history, when all woodland spirits in all their known forms, such as gnomes, goblins, leprechauns, pixies, sprites, fauns, brownies, trolls, elves, and imps, were accepted as normally as birds, bees, and butterflies. Just as fairies were part of country life, so were elves, and various early reports show a particularly strong rapport between humans and elves. These creatures were clearly less shy than the fairy folk. There are numerous reports from all over the world of elves helping humans, among them travelers in distress and lost children, whom they nurtured and returned to the frantic parents. These stories abound in Celtic, Nordic, Scandinavian, and Teutonic mythology.

It is only after St. Augustus arrived on these shores that the first schisms appeared in this alliance. The major target of Christianity was the suppression of paganism and its worship of woman, mainly in the form of the Earth Mother, but as Christianity grew stronger, the program went hand in hand with the suppression of all forms that were regarded benevolently by

Fairy Gifts, by J. A. Fitzgerald (1823?–1906), from the December 19, 1868, *Illustrated London News*

the people, including the magic ones of the hollow hills. Fairies might be able to rival the new religion, and were not fairies mainly considered to be female?

This suppression eventually embraced holy wells and streams, but it could not destroy one of the major fairy habitats, which were the barrows and tumuli where they resided. Neither could the locals be induced to destroy these ancient burial chambers for both fear and reverence for the dead within them. Sacred groves could be cut down or burned; standing stones and stone circles could be pulled down.

The Goldstone

Near where I live in Sussex, there was once a giant Neolithic circle of standing stones with a huge sarsen in the center reputed to be a fairy haunt. It appears to have had veins of gold-colored ore running down it that caught the sun and moon, leading to it being called the Goldstone, a name that has survived to this day. The park in which this stone circle stood is still called the Goldstone.

Over the years, Christian zealots broke up such stones by piling fiery woodpiles against them and splitting the red-hot stones by pouring vinegar and stale wine over them. But this turned out to be a mammoth task. Eventually giant pits were excavated and the stones toppled into them and were buried, where they await discovery. Many years ago, archaeologists tried to find the Goldstone, and a giant stone was eventually uncovered. It is now a resplendent monument that is there for all to see. There is no sign of the legendary gold seams in it.

The populace was forbidden to associate with any form of woodland spirit, so the people kept an eye on their children to ensure they did not play in the woods with elves. Gypsies could be moved away from places where people lived, but they were allowed to keep a few permanent sites in secret camps deep in the forests. Keshalyi fairies supposedly inhabit these sites.

People would leave out libations for tree spirits, who were known as dryads. Witches were said to trap these spirits within their wands and stangs to harness their power. One man by the name of Dusty Miller specialized in cutting wands and stangs with dryads in them and selling them. Oddly enough, my friend Sasha Fenton also knew Dusty well and used to marvel at his woodcarving. Somewhat reluctantly, my wife, Audrey, fell in love with one that had a prominent spiritlike head on it, and to this day she is still amazed at its power. It will twist and turn in the recipient's hands during a witchcraft ritual as though it were a divining rod!

Now, with the new religion taking hold, fairies, elves, pixies, and goblins became persona non grata, and the locals began to treat them with hostility. At this point, we do not know what ensued, but the scant records that exist, coupled with legends, folklore, and mythology, indicate that elves became bent on causing mischief.

Legend has it that young boys were enslaved as changelings and used as breeding stock if the fairy colony was in danger of dying out. Small but strong babies were favored. The fairies fed them a type of royal jelly to keep them small and to shrink them to fairy size. They say that these are "bewitched" fairies that can sometimes manifest themselves in human size, though most reports consider them to be about three feet tall. Oddly enough, supernatural beings of this size are part of the folklore of many peoples around the world.

Elf Bolts

As we know, so-called elf bolts are actually Neolithic arrowheads, but legend says that if a human victim was struck by one of them, the arrowhead would disappear magically. Thus, the elf bolts found were presumed to be of those shots that had missed their intended victims. Once struck, a victim would slowly become riddled with arthritis over the years.

After a lifetime toiling in the fields, some villagers became crippled with rheumatism and would conclude that they must have disturbed a fairy burial spot, plowed over a fairy ring by accident, or destroyed a fairy's or elf's habitat. It was also generally accepted that the elf bolt could have been fired at them to keep them away from the magical area, and in this case it had struck home.

I was told of one farm worker who had climbed onto a tumulus as a child and been struck by an elf bolt in the sole of his foot. Locals confirmed that this was so, and the elf bolt is now in the local museum. Despite the fact that the museum identified the bolt as a Neolithic arrowhead, the locals felt they knew better and the proof was that the farmer had been hurt by it! The legend was further enforced by the fact that his feet and knees were arthritic now, which was considered to be a direct result of the elf's injury to him all those years ago.

I have encountered this mixture of fact and supposition before, notably when I recorded beliefs in Berkshire. There the locals believed that the common newt, or eft, poisoned water, and no argument could persuade them otherwise. One local told me that he saw the cow drinking, and the next day it died. When he looked in the water, he saw the "critters swimmin' there."

Fairy Habitats

There is great respect among country folk for fairy footpaths, trouping paths, fairy rings, and fairy dwellings, and this has never died out. In Ireland, I was taken to numerous fairy habitats, usually by a standing stone or inside a stone circle. The locals were happy to lead me to them in broad daylight, but most of the locals refused to enter the circles, and none of them would go near them after dusk. There were too many tales of what could happen if you stayed uninvited by a fairy mound. Olivia took me to one of the most famous fairy circles in Ireland, called the Ring O' Raith, and we sat and meditated there for a while.

Apparently, far worse could befall you if you stepped into an active fairy ring even by accident, for the fairies could claim you as their own, and there was no escape. They could hold you forever if they wished, and if you were a young, attractive woman, your chances of being returned to the human world were nil. The same applied to any handsome youth, who would be offered as a mate to the fairy queen. At this point, I have to say that I can think of far worse fates! Musicians were particularly susceptible to being kidnapped in this way, and they would be given a place of honor in the fairy chambers.

Fairies and Children

This fear of being captured led to local boys and girls "pairing" whenever they ventured into the country. Even if one of the pair stepped into a fairy ring or circle of mushrooms with one foot,

Trapped in a fairy ring! (From *Peter Pan in Kensington Gardens*, 1906, illustrated by Arthur Rackham 1867–1939)

if he or she kept the other foot out, the other could pull him or her to safety. If both ended up in the ring, both would be lost. Not all who fell into the hands of the fairies remained with them. Those who were deemed suitable were given a crash course in the magical arts, and then returned to the world. There are many recorded instances confirming this, and many magical practitioners and healers have openly acknowledged having acquired their skills from the fairy folk.

"Bear the changeling child to my bower in fairy land" by Arthur Rackham, 1908. Illustration used for Shakespeare's *A Midsummer Night's Dream*.

Everyone I spoke to in Ireland stated that they knew of fairy happenings in the time of their grandparents. Usually these tales would be of milk curdling in the churn or butter going rancid, which was proof that the little ones had been offended. A worse fate would occur to any farmer who plowed too close to a barrow. Not all tales were bad, though, for alongside these stories, there were far more recounted of benefits. Ireland's legends regarding the barrow people are countless, but none more so than the various stories on changelings.

It came as a great surprise to me to find that in the 21st century, not only are fairies generally accepted and revered, but they are also feared. The most prevalent fear is that the fairies will steal a healthy human baby and bring it up as one of their own, substituting an "oaf" in its place. This oaf will grow up to be slow and dim-witted. To this day in Ireland, any mentally defective or backward male child is referred to as an "oaf." Another term that has gone out of use now is to say that someone is "touched." This means that they are slightly crazy, having been touched by or having been in touch with the fairies. A more modern expression is "Fred is out with the fairies" or "Fred is away with the fairies," which suggests that Fred is somewhat nuts! Apparently, the word "oaf" is a diminutive of the Latin "ouphe," which means a backward child, and the word was once common in France.

To avoid having their male babies stolen, the Irish still frequently dress them in pink so that the fairies will think the baby is a girl and thus leave it alone. A further precaution they took was to stoutly tie a pair of large scissors above the crib. The Irish believed that the open scissors depict the sign of the cross, which was anathema to fairies. Scissors used to be made from iron, and it is well known that if a fairy comes into contact with iron, it will die, so the scissors would certainly frighten a fairy away.

I met a seventh son of a seventh son in Clonegal, named Michael, and another called John. Both these men are revered and consulted on a regular basis. Michael confirmed that he was frequently consulted on changelings, particularly if a baby did not thrive. He confirmed the cross-dressing of babies, and the placing of iron in a crib, plus the open scissors above the baby, of course. He also told me that many women in his area would gather peony seeds while pregnant, pierce the seeds with a hot pin, thread them, and make necklaces and bracelets. They would wear these themselves prior to giving birth, and then place them around the newly born child's neck and wrists as a further defense. If a boy baby were born in a hospital, they would bring him home wrapped in a pink blanket for safety's sake. Iron pins were manufactured nearby, and these were used to pin the child's swaddling clothes together, as this would be a nasty shock to any fairy trying to pick the babe up. Doting fathers would lay their trousers across the crib when retiring for the night, as this would be a particularly potent talisman that would protect the baby.

Any baby's name would be kept secret until the child was christened or baptized, as only then would the babe be safe. As a further precaution, the child was given a false or different name, sometimes an ambiguous name that would be quite different from the child's real name. To give an idea of how this works, if you had a son called Patrick, you might call him Leslie or Bobbie, names that could be interpreted as either male or female. Only male babies were normally taken by fairies, particularly those who were fair-haired, usually when only a few days old. Young, pubescent females were also abducted if they were healthy and capable of producing good, healthy fairy stock. It was widely believed that the old village wise women, witches, and elderly healers who were skilled in the ways of charms and herbs were once young women who had been kidnapped in this way. They returned to the world of humans when they were old to practice their arts.

Dowsing
for Fairies

10

Apart from barrows, graveyards, woods, streams, and wild open spaces, another place that might yield evidence of fairies having lived in the vicinity are sacred places. The shy nature of fairies suggests that large, busy cathedrals are unlikely to interest them, but the land around out-of-the-way country chapels and churches might. Other areas that would attract such entities are old places of worship that precede Christianity.

These might be places that Native Americans occupied and where they prayed to their gods. For similar reasons, places where Australian aborigines lived can prove useful, as can places in Europe where there are ancient "henges," such as standing stones and dolmens. Having said that, Stonehenge itself is a busy place, so that's not a likely prospect for fairy hunting. However, a much better bet would be any place that has legends attached, such as wishing wells, sacred wells, sacred hills, places where miracles happened, and so on.

Try your hand at dowsing around fords, ancient droving trails, and ancient crossing points. Even if you don't find fairies or other diva entities, you will find ley lines around fords and crossroads, and that is exciting in itself.

Before you go looking for fairies, be sure to perform the exercise to open and close your chakras (see pages 54–57)

As a brief reminder, to open the chakras, you must imagine yourself gathering light from the whole universe. Then bring this light down to the crown chakra. See the crown chakra as a purple lotus (water lily) and imagine it opening and allowing the light to enter through it into your head. Then allow the light to come down inside your head and around it as far as the forehead chakra, at which point a large blue eye opens. Allow the light to come down as far as the throat, at which point a pale blue flower opens. Allow the light to come down to the heart chakra, where a bunch of green leaves opens. Allow the light to come down to the spleen chakra and let a large yellow daisy or dahlia open. Allow the light to come down to the solar plexus chakra, where a large orange marigold opens. Allow the light to come down to the base chakra, where a big red poppy opens. Then allow the light to filter down through your legs and to fill your whole body and the surrounding aura. Finish by imagining the light extending down into the bowels of the earth. Surround yourself and fill yourself with this light, and allow it to contain a little gold, as if it were subtly touched with a little of the precious metal's dust.

Don't forget to close your chakras once you have finished whatever spiritual work you are doing. To do this, reverse the opening procedure.

Dowsing Methods

There are three ways to dowse:

    With a pendulum

    With dowsing rods

    With one's hands and body

Pendulum Dowsing

Pendulum dowsing is the most popular form of dowsing because pendulums are easy to come by in New Age shops. If you can't get to a suitable shop to buy a pendulum, you can get them online via any mind, body, and spirit shop. If you don't want to go to the trouble, you can make use of any necklace that consists of a chain and a pendant. In a pinch, you can even use a heavy sewing needle threaded onto a length of cotton.

Now, hold the pendulum in one hand and place the palm of your other hand underneath it. Think "yes," and see whether your pendulum swings from side to side, back and forth, or in a circle, either clockwise or counterclockwise. Whatever movement it makes is your signal for "yes." Once you have this indication, follow the same procedure to establish your "no" signal.

Now it is a simple case of taking your pendulum to the place where you think fairies might live and mentally ask your pendulum whether the answer is yes or no. This time, just dangle the pendulum without holding your free hand underneath it. Use your mind or ask out loud whether there are fairies in the area, and wait a while to see whether the pendulum reacts. Then ask whether there have ever been fairies in the area and wait for an answer. If the answer is positive, you cannot ask the pendulum when this was, as it can respond only to a direct question that requires a yes-or-no answer. However, you can ask whether the fairies were in the area within the last fifty years, the last hundred years, the last thousand years, and so on.

If you don't get anywhere with dowsing for fairies, use the same technique to ask whether elves, dwarves, or any elemental has ever been active in the area. You can even ask for angels or spirits in general by the same method.

Rod Dowsing

Once again, you can buy dowsing rods in specialist shops or online via New Age or witchcraft sites, but if you are good with

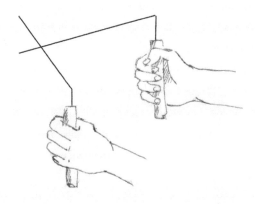

tools, it is not difficult to make a dowsing rod. You will need two metal coat hangers, two inexpensive ballpoint pens, and either a couple of lightweight wooden beads and some glue or a couple of pieces of the kind of sticky plaster that you put on a cut.

Cut each coat hanger so that you have two L-shaped rods. Take the ballpoint pens, pull the end caps off, and pull the insides out, so that all you are left with are the plastic shells. Put the short arm of one rod through the pen shell and do the same for the other. Now you will have two rods that can swing around freely while you hold the pen shells. Prevent accidents by sticking a bead on the end of each rod or by winding a piece of plaster around the end of each rod.

Once you have your rods, hold them by their pen holders and keep your fingers away from the rods themselves so that you don't restrict their movement. Now hold the rods out in front of you. Most people instinctively hold the rods far too close to their bodies, and they also place their hands much too close together. You need to have your arms fairly well outstretched so that the rods are well away from your body. You also need to keep around nine inches of space between your hands so that the rods are kept well apart.

Now you need to find the right level, because if you dangle the ends of the rods too far down, you will have too much control over them and they won't react properly. If you hold the ends up too high, the rods will swing around wildly. You need to find a point where they are still but able to move when they pick up an influence.

Now think "yes," and wait for your rods to react. They may cross, or one rod may cross over the other. Alternatively, one or both rods may swing open. In theory, the specific movement that they make will be your "yes" signal, but my experience is that any movement shows a positive result. There is no need to find a negative answer, so don't bother to ask for a "no" result. Now you can take your rods for an outing to a suitable spot, and ask the same questions discussed in the previous section on pendulum dowsing.

Hand and Body Dowsing

Hand and body dowsing is not an easy thing for a beginner to do, but anyone who is accustomed to doing psychic or spiritual work can manage it. The technique is to use your mind and body to pick up latent energies. You need to focus on feeling what is going on with your body or via your aura; this is called clairsentience. Clairsentience is the ability to feel things by psychic or spiritual means or by reaching out with your aura. Some people put their hands out as though they are feeling around in the dark, while others just walk around slowly and "quarter the area" by walking back and forth in a grid formation, all the while concentrating on what they feel and what they can pick up.

When something odd is going on in an area, whether this is a ley line or spiritual activity, the air feels different. It feels denser; there is a definite feeling that the air in the area of activity is of a higher pressure than the space that surrounds it. The space might be warmer or cooler than the surrounding air.

Once you feel something, open your mind to what it might be and see whether you can pick up a mental image. This is clairvoyance, or the ability to see things with the third eye. You might also hear music or other sounds, and this is clairaudience, which is the ability to hear things psychically.

The Elemental Realm

11

In this book and elsewhere, you will come across the term "elementals." Elementals are said to belong to the world of the diva—magical beings and energies that are invisible to most of us. They are called elementals because they personify and embody a force of nature and can be attached to fire, earth, air, and water.

Fire Elementals

These elementals prefer to occupy dry, desert places. They can be long, thin spiritual beings that change into insects or quite large animals at times. They are normally seen at sunrise or sunset or around bonfires, furnaces, and fires of all kinds.

Crystals and Stones

Fire elementals connect with red stones or stones that are associated with fire and volcanoes.

Bloodstone

Carnelian

Desert rose

Fire opal

Garnet

Hematite

Iron pyrite

Jasper

Obsidian

Ruby

These elementals bring us courage, passion, energy, success in ventures, creativity, inspiration, and breadth of vision. Fire elementals are associated with the fire signs of the zodiac, which are Aries, Leo, and Sagittarius.

Earth Elementals

Earth elementals are associated with long-lived spirit creatures called gnomes. These small spirits live in the forest or underground. Household spirits and village or countryside spirits, such as leprechauns, pixies, house elves, and brownies belong to this element.

Crystals and Stones

Earth elementals connect with earth crystals, and there are plenty of these, because so many crystals come from the living rock.

Agate

Amazonite

Aventurine

Emerald

Jet

Malachite

Rose quartz

Smoky quartz

Tiger's eye

These elementals bring us protection, security, safety, fertility, prosperity, common sense, practicality, perseverance, skill, herbal and crystal wisdom, and an affinity with animals. Earth elementals are associated with the earth signs of the zodiac: Taurus, Virgo, and Capricorn.

Air Elementals

Air elementals are fairies with wings, sylphs, and bird- or insect-like creatures. They live outdoors on hilltops, in mountainous areas, and in the wind. They can become humanoid for short periods when necessary, or they can shape-shift into bird or animal forms for very short periods. They are associated with butterflies, nymphs, and some trolls.

Crystals and Stones

Blue lace agate

Amethyst

Cinnabar

Citrine

Diamond

Lapis lazuli

Clear quartz

Sapphire

Socialite

Turquoise

These elementals give us concentration, healing powers, communication talent, and luck while traveling. Air elementals are associated with the air zodiac signs: Gemini, Libra, and Aquarius.

Water Elementals

Water elementals are associated with spirits who live in the sea or in underwater caves, and near the shores of lakes, rivers, and ponds. They also can be seen in marshy areas. They are so insubstantial that the best way to see these spirits is with your third eye—that is, in a slight clairvoyant trance.

Crystals and Stones

Aquamarine

Coral

Fluorite

Jade

Moonstone

Opal

Pearl

Milky quartz

Selenite

Tourmaline

These elementals give us intuition, inner wisdom, love, affection for nature, and peace. Water elementals are associated with the water zodiac signs: Cancer, Scorpio, and Pisces.

Fairies are uncomfortable around all metals, and even being in the vicinity of iron will kill them. Some elementals, such as gnomes and dwarves, are happy to be around metals and even make tools from them. Here are the metals that are associated with each elemental group.

Fire: Gold, brass, iron, tin

Earth: Copper, mercury, lead

Air: Mercury, copper, lead

Water: Silver, iron, tin

Flower
Fairy
Lore

12

airies are said to adore flowers and also to know all about their healing properties, so here are a few facts that I gathered after having a chat with our fairy friends! Please don't eat any of these plants or use them in any way yourself, because you might ingest something that harms you. Just enjoy reading the list, because some of the ideas here are truly bizarre. The following list is far from comprehensive, as there are many millions of plants around the world that contain medicinal properties. Some of the plants I have listed here have really weird uses.

A Few Healing Plants

Agrimony

This plant was once used to treat ulcers on the skin.

Butterbur

This plant was used for treating heart ailments, coughs, and colds. The leaves were also used as a wrapping for butter.

Cloves and Red Barstia

Both of these plants have been used in the past to treat toothaches. Oil of cloves dabbed onto a painful tooth is still a good quick fix, as is a little whisky dabbed onto the tooth—perhaps with a little more to drink for inner comfort!

Comfrey

Even today the healing properties of comfrey are well known. It can be used to treat wounds, skin conditions, and bruises, and as a laxative.

Corn Poppy or Field Poppy

This plant was once used to treat colds.

Dandelion

This plant was used as a diuretic, which is why it was said to make those who ate it wet the bed. The French name for this plant is *pis-en-lit*, which means "wet the bed"!

Evening Primrose

This plant is still used for many things, including menstrual and menopausal problems and skin ailments.

Field Scabious

This plant got its name because it is said to be a good treatment for scabs and other skin complaints.

Foxglove

The leaves of the foxglove contain digitalis, which is known to slow the heartbeat, so it was used for heart diseases such as angina or a rapid heartbeat. It is not wise to nibble these leaves, because the digitalis in them can kill.

Greater Celandine

This plant was used to treat asthma.

Ground Ivy

Once used to flavor beer, ground ivy can be used to treat chest and kidney problems.

Herb Robert

This plant was once used to treat blisters.

Mint

Various types of mint have long been used to treat a variety of conditions, especially indigestion and an upset stomach.

Musk Mallow and Marsh Mallow

We all know that marsh mallow was once an ingredient of a puffed up candy or sweetmeat, but apparently it is also useful for curing colds and flu and as an ointment.

Speedwell

This pretty little plant can be used for wounds and also as a tonic.

Stemless Thistle

It was once believed that stemless thistle cured the plague! It doesn't, so if you are unlucky enough to catch the bubonic or pneumonic plague, try tetracycline instead!

Sweet Violet

This plant can be used as a laxative and a cough medicine.

Tansy

Once used to treat worm infestations—people used to rub tansy on meat to discourage bluebottle flies!

Viper's Bugloss

This plant was said to cure snakebites! It was also used for headaches and fevers.

Watercress

This is one plant that you definitely can eat, because it is available in supermarkets. It is known to be a good source of iron.

Wild Basil

This plant is said to help relieve indigestion.

Wood Sanicle

Used to treat throat and mouth ailments.

Plants to Avoid

Deadly Nightshade or Belladonna

Not surprisingly, this plant is toxic, and while people who know what they are doing might use some parts of deadly nightshade in medicine, it is best for ordinary people to keep away from it.

Dog's Mercury

Like most euphorbia plants, dog's mercury is very poisonous.

Henbane

Animals know this plant and they avoid it, but children do sometimes nibble it. Their behavior becomes so bizarre that it was once thought that evil spirits had possessed them!

Oleander

There have been cases of accidental death (and some deaths that were not so accidental) as a result of people making kebabs and using oleander sticks for skewers.

Yew

The berries of this "graveyard tree" are poisonous enough to put those who eat them in the graveyard!

A Few Weird Plants

Celery

This is definitely nice to eat, but it was once believed to be an aphrodisiac!

Common Lungwort

Lungwort was used to treat tuberculosis, and it still is an effective treatment for coughs and inflammations.

Devil's Bit Scabious

This plant has many healing qualities, a fact that angered the devil, so he bit off some of the roots.

Forget-Me-Not

Please don't forget me! In medieval times, it was thought that this plant would prevent people from forgetting their loved ones.

Greater Celandine

Greater celandine has a history of being used to correct vision, but I don't know whether people put it in their eyes or eat it. Either way, I suggest that you leave it where it is and just admire it.

Henbane

Henbane is a well-known poison. One of its constituent parts is called "scopolamine," a poison that has a strange history. It was used by the Nazi intelligence organization Abwehr as a "truth drug" when suspected allied "spies" were interrogated during World War II. The mixture of poisons in henbane causes people who eat it to behave strangely. Children who accidentally ate it acted in such a bizarre fashion that they were deemed to be possessed by devils.

Hound's Tongue

This plant is said to stop dogs barking! It is also supposed to be good for the treatment of burns and cuts.

Lady's Mantle

The leaf of this plant has nine lobes, which some considered to be a magic number. It was sometimes fed to sheep and cattle to make them well.

Mandrake and Bryony

Both of these plants were thought to aid fertility if they were put into the bed of a woman who wanted to have children. Some bryony plants are poisonous, so it is best to leave all types of this plant alone.

Scarlet Pimpernel

This lovely little plant opens up when the sun shines and then closes up at sunset or when it is very cloudy. Scarlet pimpernel was once used in heart ailments, as it reduces adrenaline in the body, but it can both raise and lower blood pressure.

Violets

The beautiful wood violet is used in perfume. It is edible, so it is used to flavor the fillings of expensive chocolate, and the flowers are crystallized and placed on top of the chocolates. In years gone by, violets were used to flavor wine.

Wild Chicory

The petals of wild chicory are blue, but they turn pink if they are put into an ants' nest. It makes a person wonder: who would bother to put flowers into ants' nests? Someone did. Perhaps fairies amused themselves in this way and passed the knowledge on to their special human friends.

Wild Mignonette, or Dyer's Rocket

This plant was used as a cloth dye in ancient times.

Wild Teasel

This plant was once used to comb cloth to raise a nice "nap" or surface on the cloth.

Willowherb

This plant is also called the "railway plant" because it grows on waste ground and thrives beside train lines.

Conclusion

Are there fairies at the bottom of your garden? Why not? They exist wherever there is beauty and tranquility. Amid the tinkling of the waterfall, the lap of water by the lakeside, and the chirping of the birds in a woodland glade, then there, within a sea of green, they may still exist. But do not expect to come across them dancing in a ring of toadstools, for they will appear only to those privileged to see—or hear—them.

I started this quest as a skeptic, but the evidence I uncovered spanning the centuries was overwhelming, and now as a grown man I am unashamed to say that I do believe in fairies, in their original form rather than in the Victorian image of them. I shall walk the woodland paths now with a different step, and gaze upon each pond and lakeside with a different outlook. I will leave a little more fruit on each tree now, and a few more berries on each bush. This is something that I've always done for the birds, but now I will remember the fairy folk as well.

And So to Bed

But people should not sit up too late; for the time fairies like to gather round the smoldering embers is after the family are in bed, and drain the wine-cup, and drink the milk which a good house-wife always leaves for them, in case the fairies should come in and want their supper. A vessel of pure water should also be left for them to bathe in, if they like. And in all things the fairies are fond of being made much of, and flattered and attended to; and the fairy blessing will come back in return to the giver for whatever act of kindness he has done to the spirits of hill and the cave. Some unexpected good fortune or stoke of luck will come upon his house or his children; for the fairy race is not ungrateful, and is powerful over man both for good amid evil.

—LADY WILDE, *ANCIENT LEGENDS, MYSTIC CHARMS, AND SUPERSTITIONS OF IRELAND*, 1887

Other Titles in the *Plain & Simple* Series

Medicine Wheel Plain & Simple
Deborah Durbin

Meditation Plain & Simple
Lynne Lauren

Numerology Plain & Simple
Anne Christie

Palmistry Plain & Simple
Sasha Fenton

Psychic Ability Plain & Simple
Ann Caulfield

Reflexology Plain & Simple
Sonia Jones

Reiki Plain & Simple
Philip Jones

Reincarnation Plain & Simple
Jass and Krys Godly

Runes Plain & Simple
Kim Farnell

Tarot Plain & Simple
Leanna Greenaway

Totem Animals Plain & Simple
Celia M. Gunn

Wicca Plain & Simple
Leanna Greenaway

Hampton Roads Publishing Company

. . . for the evolving human spirit

Hampton Roads Publishing Company publishes books on
a variety of subjects, including spirituality, health,
and other related topics.

For a copy of our latest catalog, call (978) 465-0504 or visit our
distributor's website at *www.redwheelweiser.com*. You can also
sign up for our newsletter and special offers by going to
www.redwheelweiser.com/newsletter